Number & Letter Games

by S. Harold Collins

Illustrated by Kathy Kifer, and Dahna Solar

Published by:

Garlic Press
605 Powers St.
Eugene, OR 97402

978-0-931993-72-5
Order Number GP-072
Printed in China

www.garlicpress.com

Introduction

Number and Letter Games is part of the Beginning Sign Language Series. In **Number and Letter Games,** the finger alphabet, sign numbers, and simple, graphic signs combine to challenge the beginning signer.

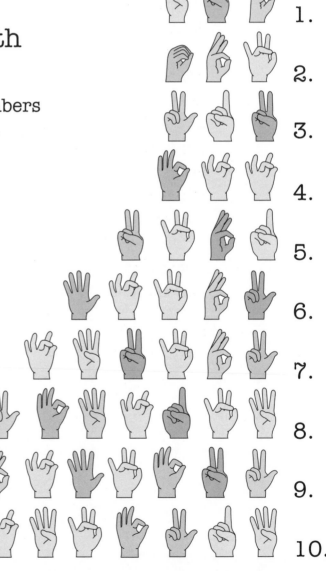

Accuracy with Numbers

Which sets of numbers are the same?

What Comes Next?

Discover the pattern.
Write the number or letter that comes next.

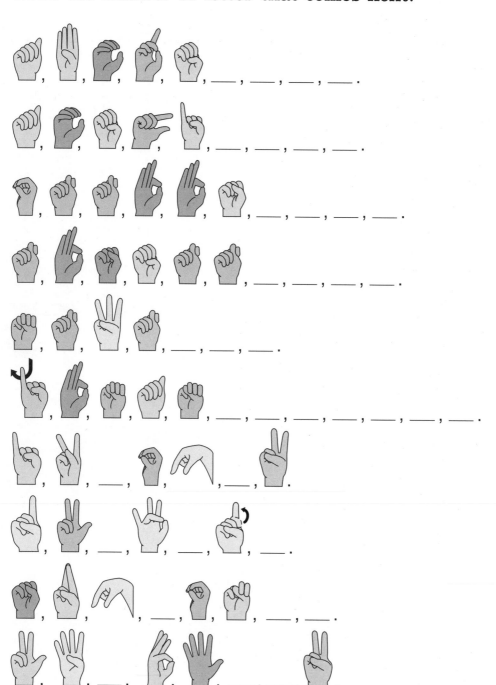

Riddles

Find the answers to these riddles.

Write the letter that comes <u>before</u> each given letter.
  With which hand should you stir your cocoa?

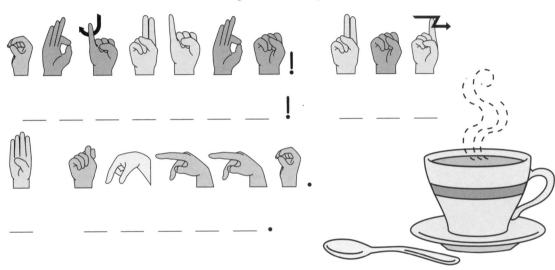

_ _ _ _ _ _ !   _ _ _ _

_ _   _ _ _ _ _ .

Write the letter that comes <u>after</u> each given letter.
  Are peanuts fattening?

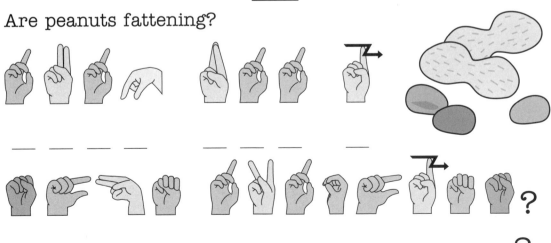

_ _ _ _   _ _ _ _ _ _ _ _ ?

Adding to 10

All but one line has at least a pair of numbers next to each other that totals 10.

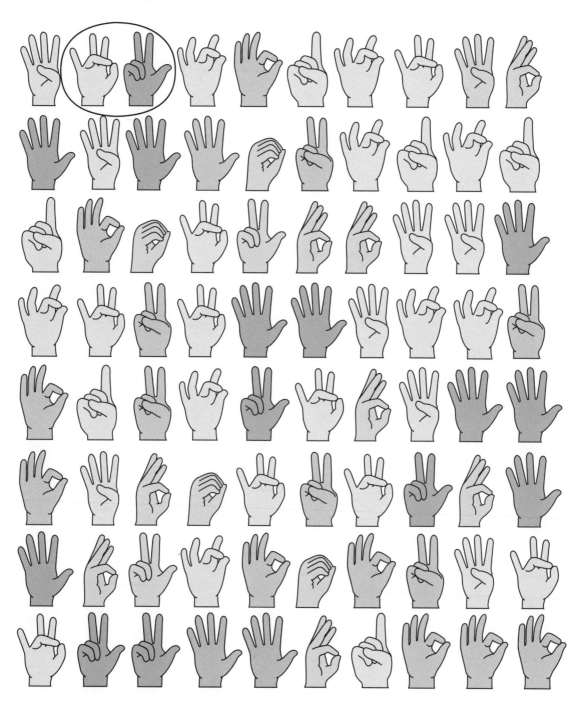

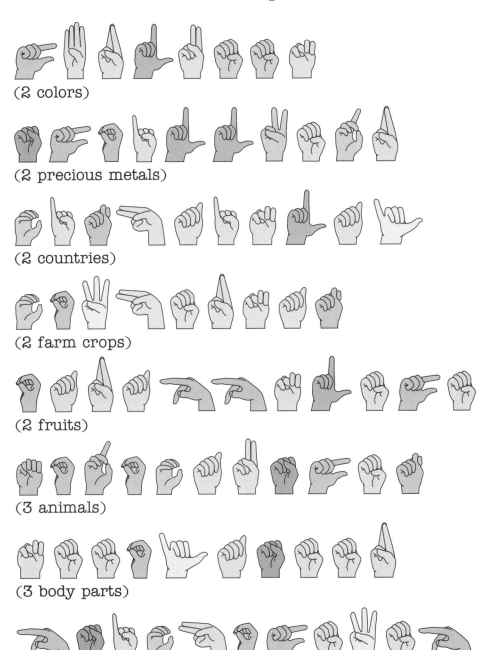

All-In-One

Two or three words have been pushed together.
Find the words with the help of the hints.

(2 colors)

(2 precious metals)

(2 countries)

(2 farm crops)

(2 fruits)

(3 animals)

(3 body parts)

(3 farm animals)

On the Border

An International monument is located on each side of th
monument is hidden in this number-letter puzzle. All pr
monument. Put all the letters together below to spell the

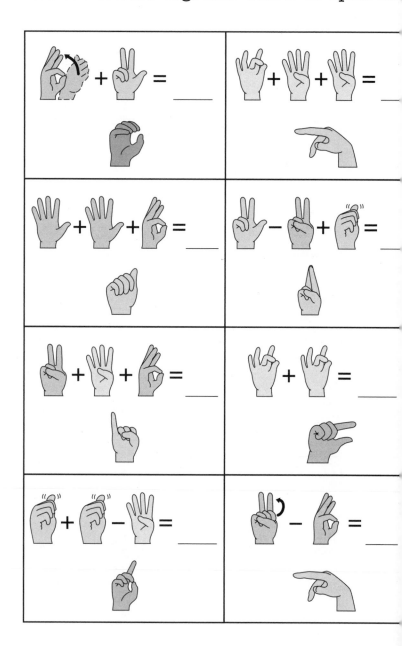

Answer __ __ __ __ __ __ __

anadian-United States border. The name of this well-known

ms with an answer of 16 contains a letter to name the

ame of the monument.

$+$ $+$ $=$ ___	$-$ $=$ ___	$+$ $=$ ___
$+$ $=$ ___	$+$ $=$ ___	$+$ $=$ ___
$-$ $=$ ___	$+$ $=$ ___	$-$ $=$ ___
$+$ $=$ ___	$+$ $-$ $=$ ___	$+$ $=$ ___

2-in-1+ Signs

The letters of two related words have been combined.
Unscramble the words and match them with their signs.

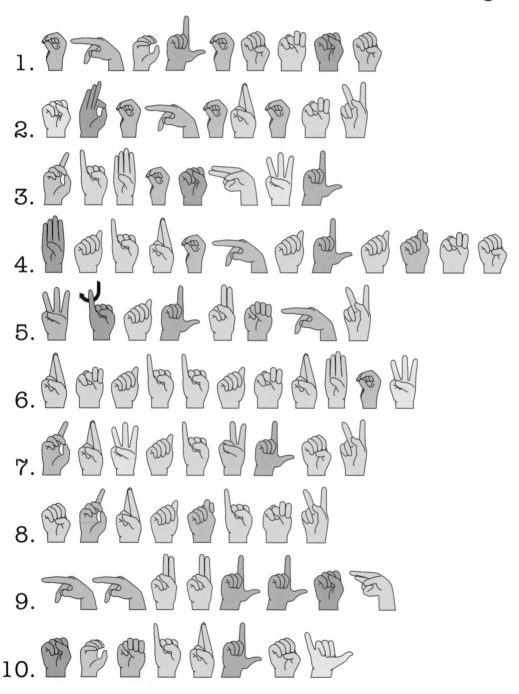

Some signs are very graphic. These pairs of signs have been chosen because they clearly demonstrate their meaning.

Sports Signs and Word Search

Find and circle the following sports on page 15. They are
spelled across, up and down, backward, diagonal and
around corners. Some sports will not be fingerspelled
with -ing endings*.

1. Tennis	5. Baseball	9. Archery
2. Skiing*	6. Golf	10. Rollerskate
3. Bowling*	7. Soccer	11. Swimming
4. Football	8. Fishing*	12. Basketball

Match each sport to its sign. Each sign clearly demon-
strates its sport.

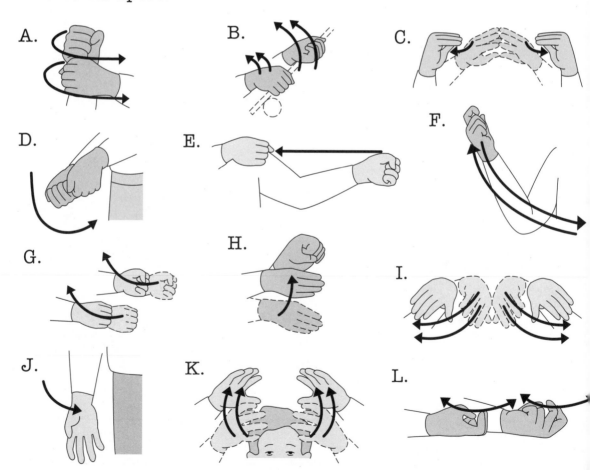

A.

B.

C.

D.

E.

F.

G.

H.

I.

J.

K.

L.

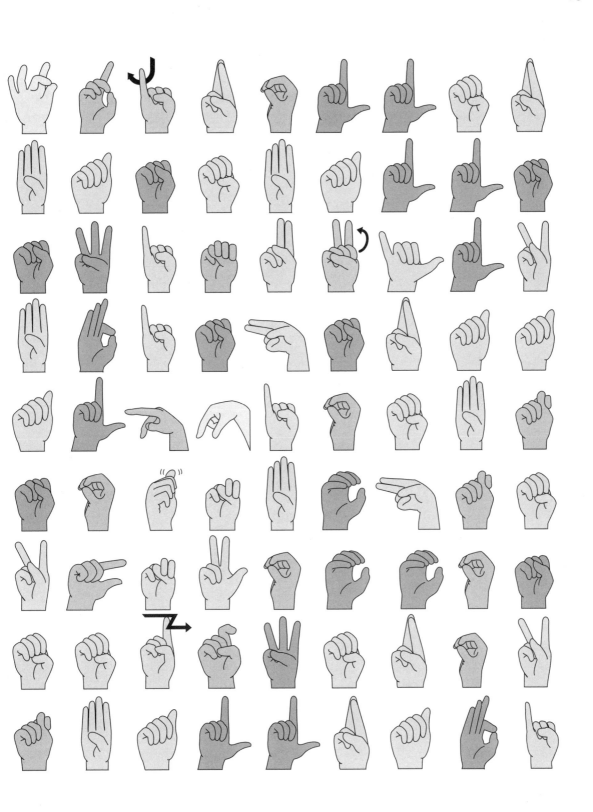

Map Skills

Can you identify the provinces in Canada and all of the states in the United States? Only the first letter of the province or state is correct. All other letters have been scrambled. Unscramble the letters, place the number of that unscrambled state or province correctly on the map.

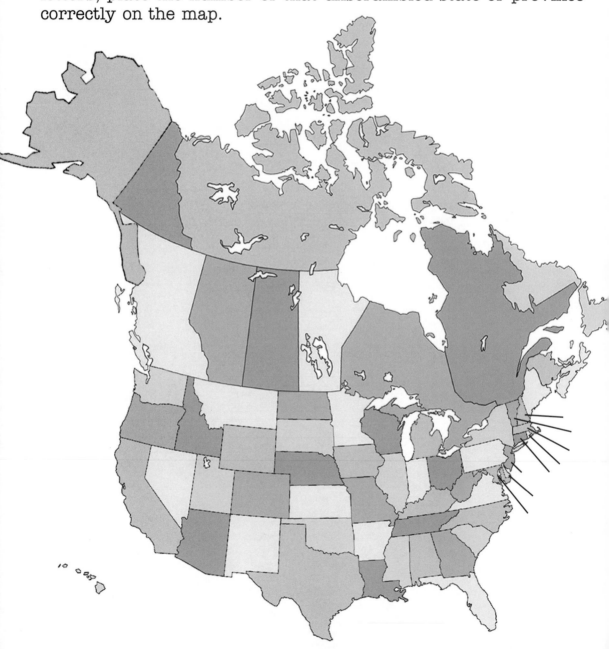

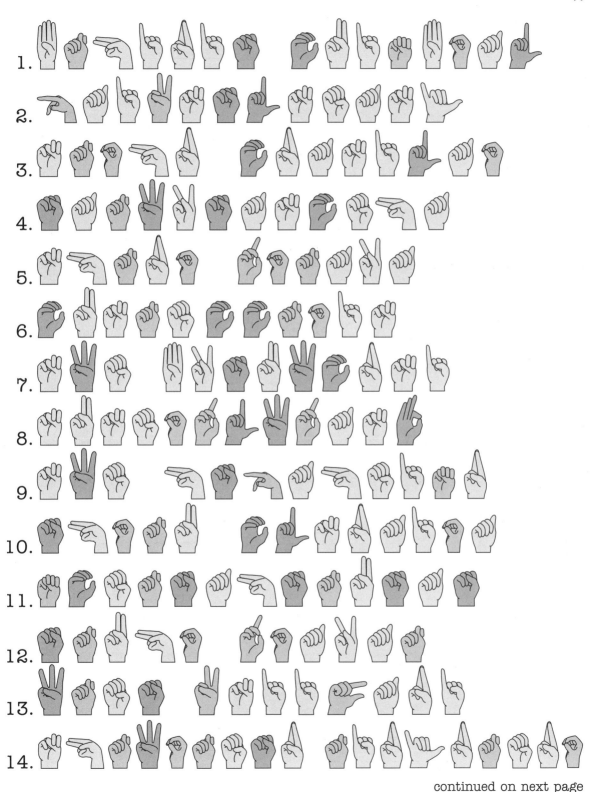

continued on next page

Map Skills continued

15.

16.

17.

18.

19.

20.

21.

22.

23.

24.

25.

26.

27.

28.

Map Skills continued

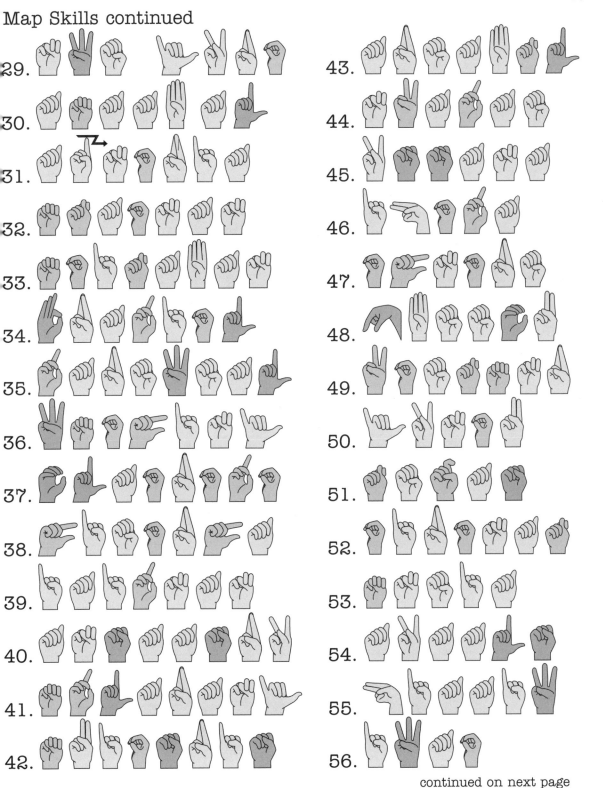

continued on next page

Map Skills continued

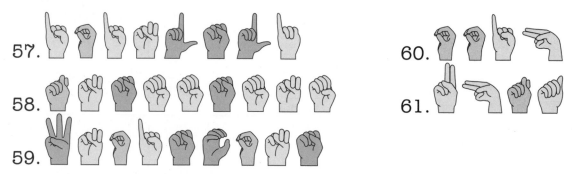

57.

58.

59.

60.

61.

Dominoes

Place the 12 dominoes below into the diagram on the next page. Two dominoes have been placed in the diagram to get you started.

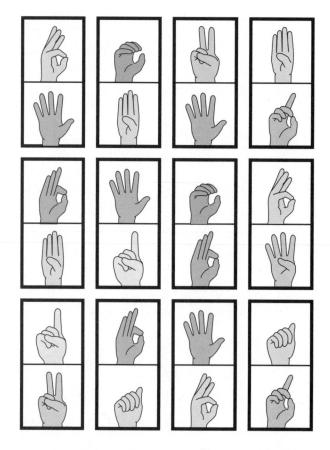

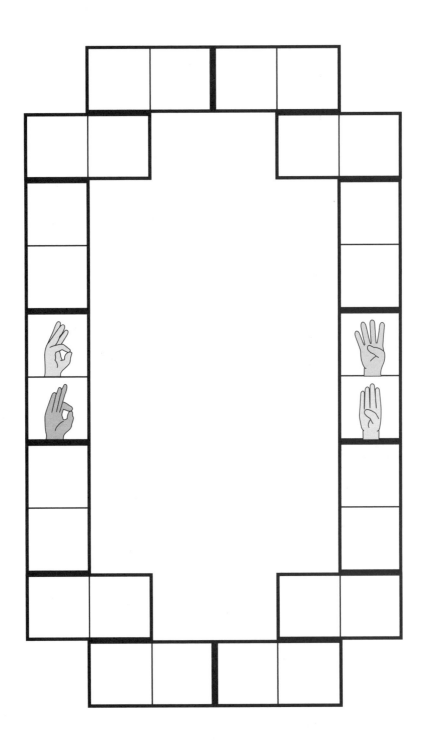

Picture This

What words or phrases do these letters, numbers, and pictures make? Match them with their correct signs.

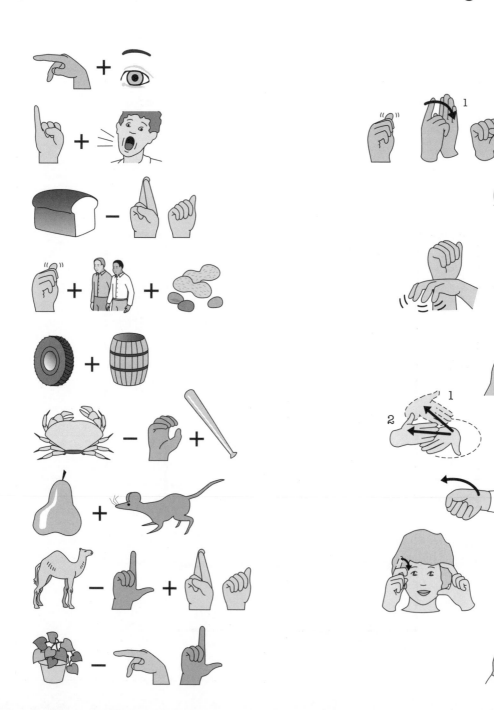

Putting It All Together

Each of these patterns can be folded into one or more
3-dimensional shapes. Find each folded possibility.

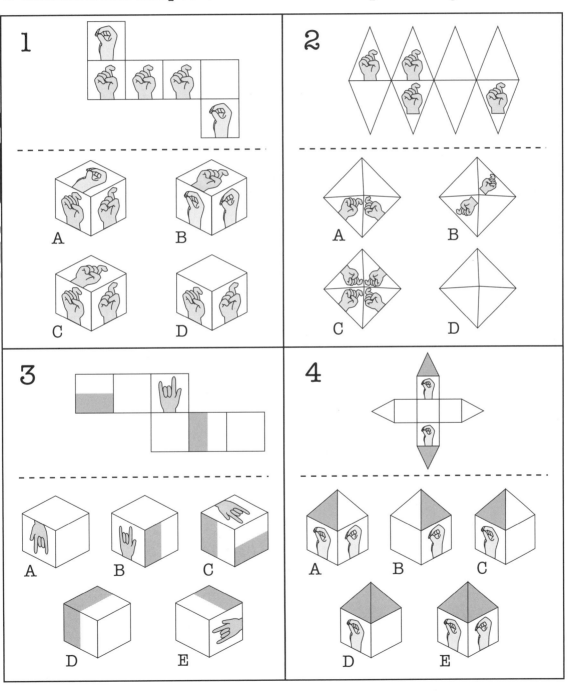

Confused Animals

Unscramble the names of these animals. Match the unscrambled animal with its sign on page 25.

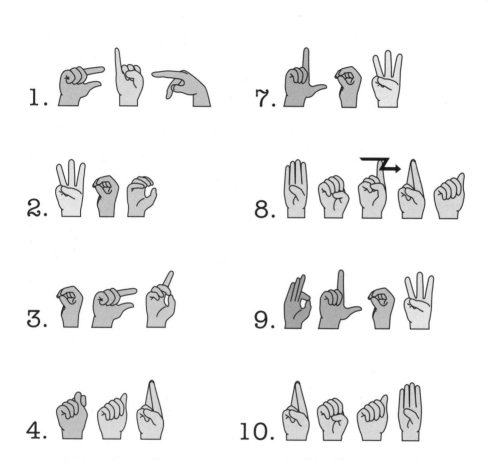

1.

2.

3.

4.

5.

6.

7.

8.

9.

10.

11.

12.

Answers

Page 4 & 5, Accuracy with Numbers

1. 420 ——————— 420
2. 067　　　　　068
3. 312 ——————— 312
4. 988　　　　　978
5. 2761　　　　2671
6. 58763　　　 58673
7. 842763 ———— 842763
8. 3948174 ——— 3948174
9. 46857923　　 46857823
10. 228479314 —— 228479314

Page 7, Riddles

N E I T H E R !　T R Y
A　S P O O N .

E V E R　　S E E　　A
T H I N　　E L E P H A N T ?

Page 8, Adding to 10

```
4 ⬭7  3⬭ 8 ⬭9  1⬭ 8 7 ⬭4  6⬭
5 4 ⬭5  5⬭ 0 ⬭2  8⬭ 1 8 1
⬭1  9⬭ 0 ⬭7  3⬭ 6 ⬭6  4⬭ 4 5
8 7 2 7 ⬭5  5⬭ 4 8 ⬭8  2⬭
⬭9  1⬭⬭2  8⬭⬭3  7⬭⬭6  4⬭⬭5  5⬭
9 ⬭4  6⬭ 0 7 2 ⬭7  3⬭ 6 5
5 6 3 8 9 0 9 2 4 7
⬭7  3⬭ 3 ⬭5  5⬭ 6 ⬭1  9⬭ 9 9
```

Page 6, What Comes Next?

A, B, C, D, E, **F**, **G**, **H**, **I**.
(Alphabet: Consecutive letters A-I)

A, C, E, G, I, **K**, **M**, **O**, **Q**.
(Alphabet: Every second letter)

O, T, T, F, F, S, **S**, **E**, **N**, **T**.
(First letters of numbers 1-10)

T, F, S, E, T, T, **F**, **S**, **E**, **T**.
(First letters of even numbers 1-20)

M, T, W, T, **F**, **S**, **S**.
(First letters of days of the week)

J, F, M, A, M, **J**, **J**, **A**, **S**, **O**, **N**, **D**.
(First letters of the months of the year)

I, K, **M**, O, Q, **S**, V.
(Skip one letter)

1, 3, **5**, 7, **9**, 11, **13**.
(Odd numbers)

S, R, Q, **P**, O, N, **M**, **L**.
(Alphabet backwards, S-L)

3, 4, **5**, 6, 5, **4**, **3**, 2.
(Up to 6, down to 2)

Page 9, All-In-One

BLUE	GREEN	
GOLD	SILVER	
ITALY	CHINA	
CORN	WHEAT	
ORANGE	APPLE	
CAT	DOG	MOUSE
NOSE	EYE	EAR
PIG	COW	SHEEP

Page 10 & 11, On the Border

19 C	16 **P**	21 C	15 O	16 **E**
16 **A**	11 R	16 **C**	18 N	16 **E**
12 I	16 **G**	16 **A**	20 U	16 **R**
16 **D**	6 P	16 **E**	16 **N**	17 10

Answer <u>P E A C E</u> <u>G A R D E N</u>

Page 14 & 15, Sports Word Search

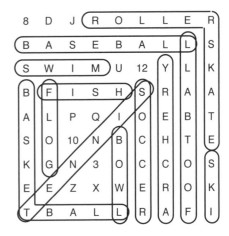

Match sport with sign

1. F	5. A	9. E
2. G	6. D	10. L
3. J	7. H	11. I
4. C	8. B	12. K

Page 12 & 13, 2-in-1 + Signs

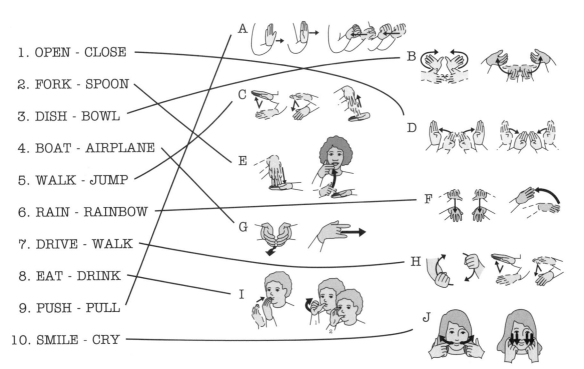

1. OPEN - CLOSE
2. FORK - SPOON
3. DISH - BOWL
4. BOAT - AIRPLANE
5. WALK - JUMP
6. RAIN - RAINBOW
7. DRIVE - WALK
8. EAT - DRINK
9. PUSH - PULL
10. SMILE - CRY

A
B
C
D
E
F
G
H
I
J

Answers

Page 16 – 20, Map Skills

1. BRITISH COLUMBIA
2. PENNSYLVANIA
3. NORTH CAROLINA
4. SASKATCHEWAN
5. NORTH DAKOTA
6. CONNECTICUT
7. NEW BRUNSWICK
8. NEWFOUNDLAND
9. NEW HAMPSHIRE
10. SOUTH CAROLINA
11. MASSACHUSETTS
12. SOUTH DAKOTA
13. WEST VIRGINIA
14. NORTHWEST TERRITORY
15. MISSISSIPPI
16. MICHIGAN
17. NEBRASKA
18. MINNESOTA
19. KENTUCKY
20. NEW JERSEY
21. LOUISIANA

22. WASHINGTON
23. CALIFORNIA
24. VIRGINIA
25. RHODE ISLAND
26. NEW MEXICO
27. NOVA SCOTIA
28. OKLAHOMA
29. NEW YORK
30. ALABAMA
31. ARIZONA
32. MONTANA
33. MANITOBA
34. FLORIDA
35. DELAWARE
36. WYOMING
37. COLORADO
38. GEORGIA
39. INDIANA
40. ARKANSAS
41. MARYLAND
42. MISSOURI

43. ALBERTA
44. NEVADA
45. KANSAS
46. IDAHO
47. OREGON
48. QUEBEC
49. VERMONT
50. YUKON
51. TEXAS
52. ONTARIO
53. MAINE
54. ALASKA
55. HAWAII
56. IOWA
57. WISCONSIN
58. TENNESSEE
59. ILLINOIS
60. OHIO
61. UTAH

Page 20 & 21, Dominoes

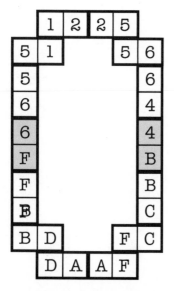

Page 22, Picture This

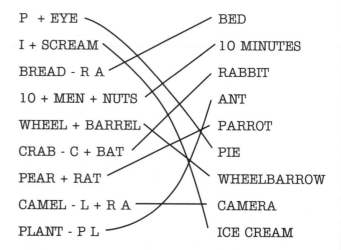

Map Skills (continued)

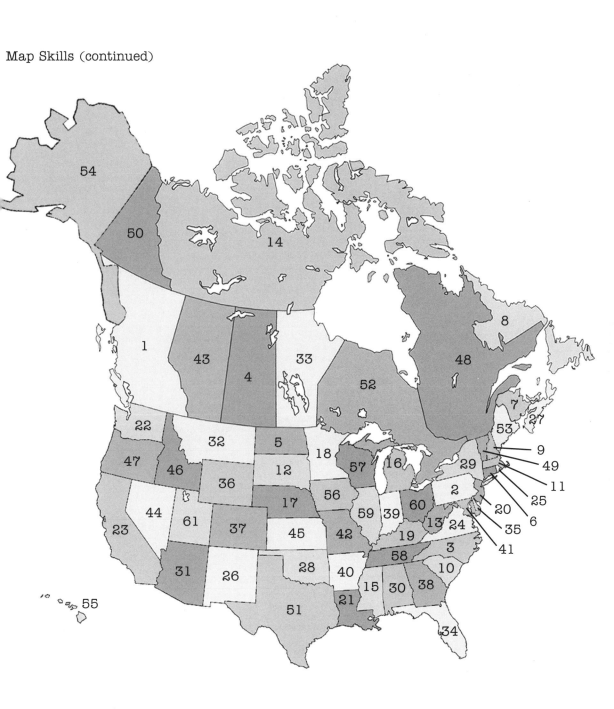

Answers

Page 23, Putting It All Together

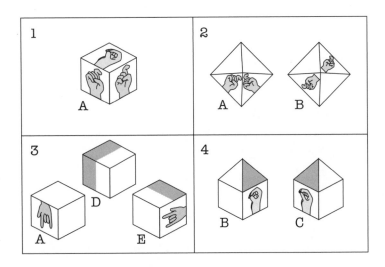

Page 24 & 25, Confused Animals

1. B   7. C
2. J   8. I
3. A   9. F
4. L   10. D
5. G   11. E
6. K   12. H

Also from Garlic Press

BEGINNING SIGN LANGUAGE SERIES

Finger Alphabet GP-046
Uses word games and activities to teach the finger alphabet.

Signing at School GP-047
Presents signs needed in a school setting.

Can I Help? Helping the Hearing Impaired in Emergency Situations
GP-057 Signs, sentences and information to help communicate with the hearing impaired.

Caring for Young Children: Signing for Day Care Providers and Sitters
GP-058 Signs for feelings, directions, activities and foods, bedtime, discipline and comfort-giving.

An Alphabet of Animal Signs
GP-065 Animal illustrations and associated signs for each letter of the alphabet.

Mother Goose in Sign
GP-066 Fully illustrated nursery rhymes.

Number and Letter Games
GP-072 Presents a variety of games involving the finger alphabet and sign numbers.

Expanded Songs in Sign
GP-005 Eleven songs in Signed English. The easy-to-follow illustrations enable you to sign along.

Foods GP-087
A colorful collection of photos with signs for 43 common foods.

Fruits & Vegetables GP-088
Thirty-nine beautiful photos with signs.

Pets, Animals & Creatures
GP-089 Seventy-seven photos with signs of pets, animals & creatures familiar to signers of all ages.

Signing at Church
GP-098 For adults and young adults. Helpful phrases, the Lord's Prayer and *John 3:16*.

Signing at Sunday School
GP-099 Phrases, songs, Bible verses and the story of Jesus clearly illustrated.

Family and Community
GP-073 Signs for relationships and family and community members in their job roles.

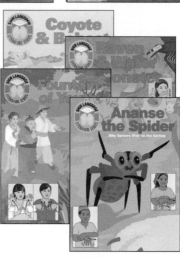

Coyote & Bobcat
GP-081 A Navajo story serving to tell how Coyote and Bobcat got their shapes.

Raven & Water Monster
GP-082 This Haida story tells how Raven gained his beautiful black color and how he brought water to the earth.

Fountain of Youth
GP-086 This Korean folk tale about neighbors shows the rewards of kindness and the folly of greed.

Ananse the Spider: Why Spiders Stay on the Ceiling
GP-085 A West African folk tale about the boastful spider Ananse and why he now hides in dark corners.

www.garlicpress.com